About the Author

Misty Barber grew up in the suburbs of Gold Coast, Australia, throughout her childhood she always used movies and books to tell her own stories. This led her to start writing *Things We Say In the Night*, to create stories of people and to express human beings.

Things We Say in The Night

Misty Barber

Things We Say in The Night

Olympia Publishers
London

www.olympiapublishers.com
OLYMPIA PAPERBACK EDITION

Copyright © Misty Barber 2023

The right of Misty Barber to be identified as author of
this work has been asserted in accordance with sections 77 and 78 of
the Copyright, Designs and Patents Act 1988.

All Rights Reserved

No reproduction, copy or transmission of this publication
may be made without written permission.
No paragraph of this publication may be reproduced,
copied or transmitted save with the written permission of the publisher,
or in accordance with the provisions
of the Copyright Act 1956 (as amended).

Any person who commits any unauthorised act in relation to
this publication may be liable to criminal
prosecution and civil claims for damage.

A CIP catalogue record for this title is
available from the British Library.

ISBN: 978-1-80074-994-8

This is a work of fiction.
Names, characters, places and incidents originate from the writer's
imagination. Any resemblance to actual persons, living or dead, is
purely coincidental.

First Published in 2023

Olympia Publishers
Tallis House
2 Tallis Street
London
EC4Y 0AB

Printed in Great Britain

Self-Identity

A search for inner peace

I wonder if the lights would take me with them,
They live in an eternal life of brightness,
No one questions their beauty,
They're just beautiful simply because they are.

Things are funny like that,
Classical music can be misunderstood as a bore
But to me it bares the way my feelings wish they could express.
It rips up the smaller part of my soul hidden from the rest,
The part where I feel the old me explores,
That part of me is stuck.

It feels like that's the only part of me that lived in eternal bliss,
I question whether I can regain the conscious, undoubtful blissfulness of what once was.

Who even am I now
If not someone that is just meant to be perceived
But not really looked at
Or judged?
When no one bothered to see,
Or at least no one wanted to,
Not yet that is.

And so
I wonder if another presence will see me as for what I am,
If there is some side of me that still can be happy,
That they will adore the parts of my soul
till they find the part of me I hope is still there.

Things have meanings
Until they don't,
Until we painfully cast away the memory of the hole it once covered.

But when we lie awake at night and lose ourselves in the meanings
What does it even do?
It gets to a point where it all doesn't feel real
And the movies and stories we so desperately try to cling onto
Drift away,
And we remember that none of it is real,
The characters are people
And the people aren't like the characters
So, what do we do?

We chase our minds around in a game
Begging for our brain to convince ourselves that it's existent.

And beyond those stories we read we throw ourselves into every single one,
Begging for them to take us as we are
So that the one place we feel safe in will accept us,

But what happens when the lights turn out,
The screens fade black,
The music and pages run out,
And all we are is inevitably,
Utterly,
Terribly,
Alone.

Ghost of A Person

Someday
I wish to appreciate existence
Without an appearance.

Loneliness

There's such an empty feeling attached to loneliness,
It grows bigger every night wishing something would join it
But loses hope by the morning when nothing comes by.

Waiting and waiting it sits
Begging for any attention
But feeling so underserving of it,
It feeds on the feeling of self-guilt and taunts the brain with how far it has cut everyone out.

But to fix this issue would be like climbing a mountain of self-doubt
Or cleaning out every word of horrible nonsense someone said to it out loud,
And to do that is much harder
Because no matter how hard it tries
There's no convincing that will prove how deserving it is of the unabundant company of at least somebody that comes around.

An observer

I look at the humans all moving around,
How do they feel anything?

How do they feel such emotion when my mouth can't feel as much to twitch upwards?
They dance around not caring who is watching
While my hands flail and stagger not daring to move a muscle.

They take risks and laugh when it goes wrong
And they don't ache inside every night questioning everything they've done wrong.

They're perfect and I'm nothing but oh so jealous of these normal people,
I'm nothing but an entity of fear and I'm scared that's all I'll ever be.

Insubstantial matters

When I look into the mirror it becomes scary to see
A face I didn't create will judge most of what I persevere.

What happens now

On occasions I feel overwhelmed,
Questioning the bane of my existence,
If my life was so destined
Beating every odd to be born
Why do I feel so useless?

Why does everything I do lead up to nothing?
Every manifesto I give up
Every indecisive moment that I take up.

It's all just taking up space,
Taking up time
Over
And over again
Till none of it consists of the beauty when I choose to wake up.

I recount memories
Deciding the way my happiness sprouts
And the sadness fills out.

Until it all collapses
And all I see are the memories
That I want to fade out.

Age of beauty

It was very abrupt the way I entered the age of beauty
As if one day I was a little girl
And the next I was being pushed off a bridge
Plunging into a pool that made me aware of everything wrong with me.

To the inch of a lobe,
To the arch of a brow,
The imperfections were everywhere,
Practically nothing perfect around.

So
I begged to dream I could change this,
Money could change this,
I could be happy if I could change this.

One less meal and I can change this,
Two less meals and I can change this,
Three less meals and I'm changing but I haven't seen anyone for days.

Three days no meals,
I dream of perfection and what it's like to be a kid again when I was unaware.

What makes this nose so ugly from yours?
What makes my smile unappealing if it is just muscles caving?

Why wasn't I prepared for the age of beauty
and what was so wrong with me to begin with?

Clone

How dimensional are my parts?
What have I torn apart and taken from afar?

Am I just a clone of all the people I've met
And if so
Where does the actual me start?

Broken

Broken rings,
Broken teapots,
They all mean the same thing,
Something torn apart that I wish I could fix.

To have people watching

I think the reason I sometimes wished my life had an audience
Was so that I was not consumed with thinking my life had no resolution.

I wanted to be a part of something bigger than me
And to be relieved with knowing that even though I was alone most of the time
There were people watching that were just the same.

Maybe if there was an audience I would get a happy ending,
A chance to live through my dreams
And not have to doubt that there's a possibility
That I won't ever find the people I'm supposed to meet
Or visit the places I must see.

Another world away

My eyes always drifted to a window,
I always found stories hidden through every crevice of the world,
To the strangers I personified
Or to the tales of fantasy I drew in the swirl of the trees.

Things were always more interesting between the cracks of the clear glass,
When I was younger this habit of mine was called troublesome
But how can I stop when everything that happens inside the clear glass
Is one second away from falling apart?

Forgive yourself

When I ponder on about the improvements I've made to myself
It's hard to look back on the many days I spent aching away losing degrees of happiness.

I didn't have anyone to save me, I did it alone
But when occasional thoughts come through about past events
It seems hard for me to acknowledge the amount of suffering I caused to the girl I used to be.

My worst enemy had once become myself and I'm not sure if I forgive that version of me yet because I still don't understand why it came about.

All I seem to know is forgiveness is a virtue and the hardest person to give it to is yourself.

How you loved me

I needed to know what it felt like to love myself
And not for the stupid teenage reason you did
But for the unbreakable bond of love that doesn't break
when I don't give into sexual advances.

I always thought love was only dependent to the status of
attractiveness you gave off,
But maybe I only saw love through your eyes,
Superficial and boring in a way that you'd find someone else
as soon as there was another face you deemed was more
appealing to you.

Insomnia

When I lie awake,
Exhaustion dripping through my bones,
I am no longer capable to drift away in fear of
Waking up and no one being there.

Unknown

At times I wish I was invisible
To live without judgement and create freely.

I hate having this persona which I craft and alter at any time,
I get sick of the past me,
I wish I could make things without bugging criticism which
hits me like a bullet and chooses to not ignore.

I longed to be anonymous and to only be perceived by those
who don't really know who I am,
I want to feel like I am not incapable of great things
compared to those that I'm surrounded by.

There are many things I would change if I could,
Starting with every single thing about me,
I was never one to try and be mysterious,
I just hated telling people things just to get tainted meanings.

I wish my brain would stop thinking because I hate the time
that passes where I'm just stuck in it,
Stuck in core memories and the feeling I get that my life
stopped long ago and whatever happens now
Is just one long depressing after mode.

Lost dreams

Why are we so afraid to do the things that might make us brave?
We live in a place where we settle rather than chase what we want like crazy.

The chasing makes us lose ourselves
While the settling gives us a missing hole of hope
The kid in us dreamed of endlessly.

Most of us stay jealous and purge on the sentence that whatever I wanted just wasn't made for me
Rather than trying and failing at the one thing that didn't scrape us away from the miserable chore of living each day in restless apathy.

Average

Everything about me felt average.

My intellect wasn't of top range
But it certainly wasn't my greatest fault.

When people met me
they didn't gush with interest,
They just thought that girl's a nice girl,
No other adjectives at all.

I wasn't show-stopping gorgeous,
But if people got the chance to know me
They might think
well her face is slightly pretty.

I wasn't admirable in my hobbies compared to what others
might classify as the best,
I had medium skill,
Medium sizes,
Which made me think
would I just be thought of as average for the rest of my life?

Would someone ever see me
Or would I just be someone you go to when there are no
other options?

Not the company you utterly desire but the company that is
reliable in which you let stick around
But only for a little while.

Recovering

Things have started to get brighter,
My head has begun to feel lighter
And that scares me half to death because I can't remember a time where things felt as easy as when I was a child.

Will this even last forever?
Because I'm afraid the next time my thoughts begin to darken
I won't make it and my dread will increase to a point where I can't take it.

The time I spent feeling inadequate has erased a lot of my time
And I feel as if I must fill the gaps from how I became so bad
To the day I decided that I wasn't just going to sit around.

I feel sorrow for that past me because she was barely scraping through a day and living without any dreams
But now because I feel different
I wish I could tell her it gets better even if I still don't fully believe it.

I still don't know if my head is normal
But trying to clear it from its evil thoughts is all I really want

Because one day I hope to not be so socially anxious,
I hope I can eat something and not have to hate the way it sits in my stomach,
I wish that all these things can erase themselves one day because nobody deserves to feel suffering
Coming from their own mind.

We are all capable of change and just going through the motions is not a way for us all to hide,
We can feel,
We can laugh and cry and dance
Because we can all achieve the wildest of things as long as we try.

I've spent a lot of days feeling like nothing
But I don't want to do that anymore because there are so many things I want to try,
Like falling in love,
Discovering a new food I like
Or the feeling I might get one day when I know what it's like to finally achieve all that I so desperately want in life.

A party you don't want to be at

I'm so sick of trying in a room of people just to get written off,
What was the reason for so many distained looks to be thrown my way?

Why was my figure to be ignored?
If I just stood here the whole night would I even talk?

Would I have to ignore my morals in order to fit in just a little bit more?

Why am I at a party I don't want to be at?
Why does anyone go to a party they don't want to be at?
Is it to stand there intoxicated even when knowing it's still not enough?

People laugh
While one face remains unchanging,
you try to stay in the moment
but the drinking is moving time too rapidly.

You sit on a dusty couch wishing you had the ability to attract,
Craving to be something more and willing away the ache of dread rested deep in your belly

As it chooses to not let the brain be consumed with a single good thought.

So,
You remind yourself this is why I hate parties
But you know for a fact
That if people noticed you
You would love it here a whole lot more.

Changing

I feel as if I've changed too much over the months,
Too much in such little time that I barely recognise any piece of me.

I don't even feel like a person anymore,
I feel like a worn-out shell of a person begging for something to appear that makes me want to be here.

I'm sick of wanting things that keep me up at night,
And waking up too tired after barely sleeping because my chest feels too tight.

I'm sick of not experiencing real connections and being so alone,
Because I just want people near me,
But it's as if anytime I open my mouth
I'm speaking another language that no one else can understand.

I've come to realise it's hard to come across people who can accept you in ways you can't yourself,
But for seconds at a time I beg my entire existence to just help me find one body
That adores me in ways no one else had bothered to before.

Five a.m.

It's in these moments
When it's five a.m.
And the coffee warms my nose
That I truly feel the simplicity in waking up alone.

Nothing else matters more in that moment,
The whole world is asleep
And my heart is the only one beating.

Alternate

You wrote yourself in stories
The same way people had written you out.

You changed what you looked like
And everything single thing about your personality.

It hurt that you despised every fraction of yourself
But you thought
Maybe in your alternate universe
People would want to stick around.

Disconnected

I guess it doesn't really matter how many people can be in your space,
When no one knows who you are beyond layers that most people don't face.

The girl I used to be

I wanted to love the things I used to adore every night,
I wished I had the same dreams that most thought were too unreachable.

I wanted to be the girl I used to be,
So uncaring and naïve,
I wanted her back,
The parts of her that thought she could achieve nearly anything.

She's gone now and what saddens me
Is that I'll never be her again
Because too many things have happened from that time to now,
But I beg for forgiveness from her because I'm afraid
I put her through too many things that she didn't need to experience.

What I wanted

I wanted to drown myself in the parts of me that weren't so troubled,
I wanted to down whatever drink I could to fix any damage that had been done.

I wanted someone there because no one else ever was
More importantly I wanted to be someone that mattered
And to live in a head that didn't think so much.

What they don't tell you

They don't tell you when you grow up how much heavier you brain feels with every year,
They don't tell you how much you exhaust yourself in loops you've been through a million times before.

They tell you to pick a dream when you're young
But to settle for something else as soon as you mature enough.

They don't tell you how much others will change
And the moments that pass where everyone hates each other,
I wish they'd told me these things so I could have gripped onto my childhood a little bit harder.

I wish they told you that it's okay to be nothing that anyone expected
And that you weren't doing something wrong by simply existing.

Everyone leaves you raw,
Alone
And shattered in pieces
Till we are supposed to accept that that was a good thing,

Something to learn from.

That you're a strong person because of this,
When you could have experienced things as someone that
didn't feel broken and torn,
And was just happy to be here.

Hatred

I hated the periods of time that I felt rage for everything I saw,
It felt ugly and I wanted to be the caring person everyone thought I was.

It was like I was living a lie because no one knew who I was besides from the things they perceived of me,
I was too afraid to say what I meant and do as I pleased
Which made me feel isolated because I was the only one who knew who I actually remained to be.

I loathed myself,
So
I dug that part down and tried not to let anyone catch a glimpse of
The real shell of decay of my soul
That was laced deep and hidden
For the world not to see.

Reshaping

People grow and reshape,
Sometimes unintentionally for they just didn't want to be
who they had always been.

Others tend to make us feel this way
We don't have to change but when we feel the need
I wish we didn't change the one thing about us
That separated us from being just like everyone else.

I wish we could all revert to the childlike selves we were once,
Because everyone was so utterly unique
Before the world told them they couldn't be.

Pure

I wanted to wipe the crease in your brows and hug you clean,
Those horrible thoughts were buried through the lines of your face,
A face that was always a million worlds away.

You felt gross and inhumane
For you shamed yourself every second of every day
But if I could hold you and take all the pain away
Then I'd sell my soul just to do it plenty times again
Just to erase
Every single bad thought that was fed to your brain.

You were abundantly pure and deserving and to see you get thrown away the second you came into this world,
Well, it was one of the biggest tragedies.

A stare

A stare can say a million words,
A story,
A feeling,
Destruction and falling in love.

Sometimes it's blank as you stare at barely anything,
Demanding that you were somewhere else,
At the little place you kept in a secret hatchet in your mind,
The place no one knew of where you didn't have to hide.

You spoke a loud
And did the things you always longed to do without anybody about,
You fell in love with characters you made up in your head,
Created people that didn't question who you were before accepting you.

Then a clearing of a throat snapped you out,
Took you back and reminded you that this is really where you are now,
Stuck in a place where people dislike you,
Where you're too afraid to do anything other than blend in
And cover the thoughts you could never have the courage to say.

In moments

Sometimes in moments of fast pacing cars,
And incandescent stars,
I think the world brought me illustrations to narrate,
To sew a string of words together that could fit the scene before me.

Sometimes the words align and everything's perfect
And my mind thanks whatever thought brought those words alive.

Tunnel vision

I hated looking at people just for them to not look back,
So I tuned it all away,
Made my vision a tunnel to keep everyone out.

I was so invisible to anything that had a heart,
So I stopped trying
And gave up hope that anyone noticed if I was still breathing.

The stars you can't touch

When I look in the mirror on days where my head hung low
All I see awaiting me
Are days filled of misery
And pining over people who want nothing to do with me.

People that I hang in stars above me only to look at
So far away and hard to find.

I'd admire them and watch from a distance
But to see them up close and touch their glow,
Well, that is something unforeseeable to the ordinary people
that don't have beautiful qualities.

Stars touch other stars and don't look down at the people
that beg to be near them
And I'm just a beggar hoping I'm worth more than what I've
always thought.

Lonely in the corner

When I sit in a classroom alone
I wonder how this happened to me,
How I managed to find no one
And changed completely.

Did I glad rap my bubble
Or turn hideous to every outsider?

How did I manage to spend this many years in the same confined space and not have a single person with a promising connection?
I dreamed of days where I wasn't alone
And filled my thoughts with memories of people I didn't know,
Made up friends when it was only ever me talking to myself.

Sometimes I would go days without my mouth opening,
The dryness sticking my mouth together like hot glue,
My voice growing crackly every minute that went by where no one had said a single thing directed at me.

Sitting in my corner
I contemplate on how I got here,
So unwanted and secluded
Questioning whether I liked my own company
Or if it had always been this way and I just adapted.

Run

I used to think if I ran fast enough
I could escape the torture of living trapped beneath everyone's weight,
But all of a sudden I'm running slower and I'm not sure if it's because reality has sunk in
Or my legs have given out and rather drown in this sadness
Then chase the freedom land that was never really there to begin with.

This place I chased lived without people and the expectations and thoughts that you were always letting someone down,
It was untouchable to anyone who couldn't see it
And only existed to those who wanted to seek it.

When we leave

To escape is easier to plan than do,
To leave the place you hated eternally
Has got a hold on you that you can't shake out.

The place you went to school,
The place you had your first date,
Or the spots you created all over town.

Every inch had a meaning
And was impossible to leave behind,
But you can't grow without the change
And saying goodbye is one the hardest things
Because what if we never get any of these memories back?

Leaving it all behind in hopes you get one thing right,
That every fault you had here would be cherished somewhere else,
The place that you could make your own,
Separate from the things that you were told.

Café seat

While I sit in a café
And the sky brings tear drops down,
A drink too sweet lightens my tongue,
My head choosing to be silent for once.

It's easy in these moments
to forget all the ways
I've never been loved.

It comes reeling back to me almost as instantly as it is forgotten,
But for a second it's bliss
To have a mind without thoughts
And to enjoy the simplicity in where you are.

A person with no meaning

Everything was slipping out of my grasp,
There wasn't a second in place that I could hold onto
Or to the things I cherished the most.

It was all leaving
And I was left standing alone
Trying to orchestrate what was left in this miserable life I called my own.

I begged anyone near to give back the things I loved so dearly
But no one heard,
They pushed me aside and I became stranded.

Does a person without their belongings have any meaning
Or was there now nothing to me?

Wasting time

There are moments in my existence where I dread every second,
My body weightless and mind a mess,
Glued to a bed I lie and indulge in every thought that went unsaid
And every person that left as quickly as they came.

In these instants time is exhausting and feels draining to the core
And any lyric or line I had written felt unnatural and made me want to rewire my mind
To be someone who was exceptionally unique and loved from afar.

My tiny insignificant life

My tiny insignificant life,
Was a path with not much change,
Not enough people,
Or things I could have attained.

It was one that would certainly bore
And a life full of regret of not being who I wanted,
Being a watcher full of envy for these people that shone for everyone to admire.

The inconsequential being I was
Lived in the shadows of everyone I met
And let every scary creature stomp all over me taking everything they fancied away from me.

I never stopped them, instead I began to welcome them and not put up a fight,
Let them take anything they wanted because I just wanted to float away most of the time.

Words on a page

I could write as much as I want
And it would still be meaningless,
A bunch of gibberish written without any thought.

A construction of hollow words not enough to attract any readers,
But they held my own sense of being that begged anyone to relate.

A cinema viewing

I often watch people through the looking glass,
Guess their name
Or what their life is kind of like.

I wonder if they think about me,
The girl inside the window watching them
Who goes through her days without any vital change
Ever so curious,
Guess I'll never know.

I question upon if they think that someone might be speculating about them,
Or if anyone's ever done that to me,
But most of the time I feel invisible,
Just like a cinema screen showcasing everyone else that walks past.

Out of breath

Breathing didn't come easy to me,
My lungs never figured out how to properly work,
Any pill should have fixed things by now
But they only ever dissolved,
Leaving things unchanged.

My withdraws were numbered
And singled out as they came,
I wondered if that's why my brain ran slow and lacked determination
And self-growth.

Maybe it was because the air in me was selfish
And didn't feel the need to try,
So it just slowly died till I could live without it.

Compliments you don't receive

My level of self-esteem was never constant
Or stagnant,
It came and went in waves of satisfaction.

People always talked about how much we should love ourselves
But what if all we see is ugly flesh we want to rip off,
I wanted to feel pretty,
Not in a way that was unique and took a while for people to perceive,
But in a universal way that had no one questioning whether or not,
I was someone that most would desire.

It wasn't as if I got called ugly often,
It was just the silence that was so very loud
And the words I always wanted someone to say to me
Were words never spoken.

This made me grow in constant jealousy that I was made like this,
Because who wants to look like someone that just gets ignored.

Living through the pages

I never lived a single day in my perspective,
My days were long and plain with no rushing activity,
I lived through characters that were nothing like me,
Dug myself into their lives and imagined what it was like.

I did it to feel something,
Because without the plot lines that came from someone else's restless head,
I had nothing and I was afraid to live without these imaginary friends.

People told me I indulged too much in stuff that wasn't real
But I found myself questioning how they liked to exist in a world that only let them down
And accepted it rather than turning to a place where things are exactly how you want them to be,
A place where people treat you like you matter and to have someone that loves you,
Beyond their selfish desires,
But because they saw you for everything you are.

Even if these things were not palpable when reality was placed in front of my viewing
There was not a sense of care I could find,
I would always remain in some part of these dreams
And that was the one thing no one could take away from me.

I hate when my eyes are wet

Tears were hard for me to achieve,
My eyes were all dried up,
They always had been.

At certain times it would flow like an occasional storm,
These storms lasted hours and were caused by a slow build up,
But when they finally let up
It started to rain down quieter.

At a young age I was taught how annoying other people find your tears,
So I never showed anyone what I looked like when I cried
I always swallowed them down anytime they threatened to come out,
But sometimes your emotions don't care about your lack of showing vulnerability
And your storm thunders loud for everyone to see.

Everyone's waiting

Expectations were always something I hated,
Everyone was always in my own personal waiting room,
Waiting for me to do something
Or fulfil some lifelong dream.

I just wanted to stand still
And let myself scream,
Listen to what I actually wanted instead of what everyone else wanted from me,
I wanted to kick back every person that watched
And grew impatient with my lack to succeed.

What if everyone stood still for seconds at a time?
I think we deserved that much peace,
To not hear noise every once in a while
Or be held down like prisoners to our own life.

Imperfect bones

There wasn't a time I could recognise where I started to notice things like
How to check the number your body is rated,
Or number of bones that were in your way of having perfect edges,
Lines,
And colour-ins.

Weight was no longer nothing,
It was everything,
And the girls that were drawn perfectly were pointed out
Enough to make the outliers nearly kill themselves in order to be painted in their special way.

The outliers were drawn with unwanted pencils and tired artists,
Sculpted and crafted with no effort
And were often used to the feeling of not being chosen.

I was an imperfect sculpture with rough edges and incomplete stripes
And it was all anyone ever seemed to care about.

Paint me pretty

I thought a bucket of paint could make me pretty
But it just coated me in a new colour
Which didn't make me any more appealing.

So eventually I tried every colour
And mixed every shade together,
None of it worked,
I was unhappy and no one thought I was pretty.

One day I stopped painting myself
And let my natural colours scrape their way through,
I stopped buying buckets of colours
Because they were only causing damage,
Every person only said they always hated whatever pigment I picked out.

I was a dull person with little colour
But it seemed that even at times when I was vibrant
Still no one appreciated me.

Dirty

The more I washed myself
I believed it meant the more I could scrub myself clean,
Erase every bad memory
Just to be refreshed and seen.

I thought I was dirty
Even when I was drowning in fragrance,
Because every crack of me was still filled with plain misery
And repressed dreams.

I could burn myself in boiling water
And it still wasn't enough to make me feel the heat,
It left noticeable marks
Which was the only telling thing
That I was still a heart beating.

Somebody else

Most of my dreams were spent being other people,
I basked in what it felt like to operate differently
And fantasied things I've never done through these made-up creatures.

They got everything I never experienced,
These individuals had long detailed love stories,
Tales of sneaking out and hiding kisses behind trees,
Their beauty was unmatched,
bodies crafted perfectly.

All their aspirations came true
And I was stuck pretending I had this,
That I was them.

I never imagined being myself
Because in the blink of an eye I thought I could change into them
And be someone that was worth living.

Nobodies around

There was a difference between liking your own company
And being truly lonely,
Sometimes I can't feel it
But other times it's too difficult to ignore
Because when there isn't at least one person you can go to,
Is it that fun to be alone
On the nights you can't sleep?

Climb your self-doubt

There were invisible mountains I climbed
That no one could see,
But they took all my courage
And took ages to hike.

Others couldn't see these elevations
Because I guess to others they were flat lands,
But to me these peaks were made up of simple things
Like managing to talk to someone I didn't know
Without my voice wavering,
Or going to the unknown
Taking a chance in hopes it works out.

I had hidden at the bottom of the hill for so long
That I realised that nothing came from not escaping our own minds,
So I leaped every rock that was in the way,
Because I was sick of being someone that lingered in fear,
I wanted to be there spinning from the highest point of my mountain
And remove myself from any distress that threatened me.

Think badly about yourself

People had tricked me into thinking I should hate things
That I actually liked about myself,
Anytime there was a chance for self-discovery
Everyone tore me down,
Said I was egotistical for trying to think I had more than a little value.

Small things that I couldn't understand
Bothered people,
Made them mad with fury,
Supposed friends hated when you had some idea about who you were
But also when you were too dependent.

I could never grasp the level of control people thought they were entitled to
On an individual's life,
It was always leaving specks of constant envy lurking around.

The whole world was shut down because they wanted you to need something from people,
Just so that they could play the act of the one that's put together.

What do I have to do

I always thought if I had or dropped something
It would make me happy,
But the results were always severely underwhelming
And I couldn't work out why the chemical balance in my brain
Was always incorrect,
Making me question when this feeling would finally leave me.

I spent most of days picturing my life through the other side
Where I left things in the past when I was supposed to,
And stayed a little longer for the things I wasn't ready to give up,
Or imagining that someone was there
To tell me what decisions I would come to regret.

Anything to know what path to take so that my mind was composed of blissful thought
Instead of gloomy clouds
So that I don't have to be consumed by the idea that someone trespassed into my head
And made me too self-aware.

Part time

I'm afraid this is all I'll ever be
Stuck serving others
And counting my money
Till I can be free.

There was no time to even think,
My whole body just ached with desperate need
To be something more than what was considered of me.

It saddened me that I didn't feel like I had another year left of my young life,
Where I could relax and not have to be anywhere,
Will I just walk around with sore feet
And give to people
Who don't care to show any sort of decency?

I had no time to make memories,
My adolescence was running out
While all I did was crumble under my breath
Hoping that this would all be worth it.

To be fifteen again

Can we go back to the old days
When everything was light?
As we had fun getting up to things in the night
And we liked the music we played.

I was stuck grieving over the time I spent summer of being fifteen,
In the moments where nothing was decided,
The future could wait,
Things were new
And we still had exciting infatuations.

Now we're stuck being people we don't want to be,
With an alarming sense of nostalgia
That convinces us not a thing will ever amount to what has already been.

People pleaser

There was nothing I hated more than being a people pleaser,
I no longer was able to do what was best for me,
Every need that anyone claimed I had to fulfil them
Instantly made me give in,
Even when it ruined everything in my life,
I did it all to avoid awful confrontation
And the idea that I was an inconvenience to mankind.

It was a fault I had,
Never being able to let even the horrible ones down
Because it lit a sign on my back that let everyone know
They could walk all over me,
So much so that
I was constantly glued to the ground
And surrendering without bothering to stand.

I was just a dog to everyone around,
Especially when they found out I couldn't say no,
They ordered my arms,
legs and mind
Which forced me to be stuck in my incapability to stick up
for my identity.

Wait

I was always in a waiting game,
Waiting till I wrote something really great,
Waiting till I met someone,
Waiting till I was content with my reflection
And till things would become simple again.

Comfort

Comfort was what I was desperately chasing to find,
Wistful for it each minute
Because for the time that passed where I was alone with my thoughts
Was time that I rarely let be existent.

Silence was too loud
And my ears grew sensitive to the muffled sound,
So I fought to find the happy noise of laughter in shows
Where characters had exciting experiences.

I just so badly wanted to be enveloped into these nostalgic things,
Or to have an immature brain that was still as trusting.

Half closed

Why do my eyes always hurt?
The creases of my lids continuously drooping
Uncomfortably low,
My eyes irritated
like they were the day before.

Why couldn't my brain stop being paranoid
So I could get at least one night's sleep
And not be unprepared for the blinding morning lights
That hit my irises harshly?

It made me give up in trying to rest
Since it only ever came again.

Worry

The unsettling was hidden through planks on the ground,
You just had to lurk around to grasp it
Because once it was seen
It would beg to crawl into your skin
To make you afraid of everything in sight.

Can I be her?

She smiled a lot,
I noticed,
It seemed like she was the epitome of joy
And was guaranteed everlasting happiness,
She effortlessly got along with people and it made me infinitely jealous.

Sometimes I wished I was her
Because our lives seemed so contrastingly different,
Just by her personality alone
You could tell that she never had to worry
About there being no one to talk to
When a conversation was needed the most.

Of course she had probably faced hardships
But just by her radiance
You could tell she enjoyed her world.

Touch starved

All day long the ghost of air
Above my skin became the only sensation I could feel,
It rose the hair that it homed
And grew cold because it had been abandoned.

The one thing that would send the ghost away
Was human touch,
Which it had long forgotten the feeling of,
It ached more as the days went by,
Still too conscious of every place that hadn't had heat.

As soon as someone came by and wrapped their hands
around any part of me,
Like a blanket
My skin would cave and surrender
Because all it ever wanted was for someone to show remorse
And take care of it
In a way where it could be soothed by touches that didn't
leave colours and marks.

Tore myself down

No one could forgive me for the damage I had done to myself,
Only I was to blame for making my skin hallow and beating my mind in,
I was not a scientist so I couldn't fix the chemical imbalance
But for a short while it could be eased
And my scars were forgotten.

When I looked into a shard of glass
Reflecting a face that was staring back,
It flashed me back to who I was when growing up so out of reach
And I cried for her future,
The cards I set out for her to receive.

She'd cry if she saw who she turned out to be,
Bandaged up like a broken-down statue,
I tried to get better to make things easier for the young child
But forgetting was hard
And my mind wished that I didn't have to mature so fast.

Why couldn't I hold onto careless trivial matters
Instead of burning away my insides
Seconds at a time.

The best years of your life

I'm not sure what to make of the time I'm in,
There weren't enough fingers on my hand that I could count
The number of people that told me these were going to be
the best years of my life.

If it were I had no hope,
Because these years were not fun
And took everything out of me,
I'm not sure who came up with the philosophy
And imprinted it on anyone they could
But being a teenager was not like a movie,
Rather one long uneventful episode of being anxious.

Being a teenager now
Meant giving up on fantasies,
Losing yourself to daydreams
And learning what it's like to be alone.

Walking through hallways filled with people you don't know,
Gaining disorders
And the inability to feel in control.

Feeling everything you've never felt
But in the worst possible way
And letting people ruin you and take your innocence away.

Try hard

Maybe I'm trying too hard to have qualities
That people would like in me,
But I craved to be likeable
So that people didn't find out how horrid my parts were.

My body became exhausted
Any time there was some sort of contact to be made,
I tried harder than everyone else,
Fought through stutters and uncertainty
To cycle out my bad traits
And put forward a person that people would want to converse with.

The only troubles I was facing
Was that it was getting increasingly impossible to mask this persona
But no one would adore me if I just played the role of my true self.

Trapped

I let things ruin me
Because I'm too afraid to admit what I wish would change,
So, my feet stand still and let it all fall over me
Till I'm no longer living the way I want to,
I'm just doing the things everyone needs.

On this day I am simply a person with no control,
With an eternal soundtrack of screams in my mind
For all the times I've been stuck in this routine.

In a world of ant eaters

Hours of sleep I haven't had
Are made noticeable as they paint a simple shade under my eyes,
I get out of my bed
Noticing the indifference I make
Regretting decisions
And cringing at my idly made delusions.

My face droops down
But I spend days living as an ant
Covered from the surface
Looking at people who think I'm invisible.

A Heart That Hurts

I used to be a hopeless romantic

I was never one to be in love,
Feelings were always out of reach for me
And other's delightful sappiness only made me feel robotic.

But for moments at a time, I would read pages after pages of romantic literature,
I guess I used to wish that I was them
But I grew accustomed to the idea of such pureness never truly developing for a person like me.

For I changed psychically and couldn't help but see,
Only the utterly beautiful experienced such things
And it seemed like I already didn't fit anyone's criteria,
I was just an outlier when I really didn't wish to be.

Promises that you don't pinkie swear

"When I open my eyes I wanna see you."

I told you,
"You don't mean that."

You just smiled at me saying
"See that's it, when I'm with you I don't have to think I can just say."

I never believed you
Why me?

Eventually time would not be friendly to us
And I was proven right again,
Except you were the one thing I didn't want to be right about.

Love me

My skin burns when you touch me,
You use me every night
But my heart longs forever for you.

You're in love with her,
That you can't see
the burning mess my body is whenever you're near.

I wish you would see me,
I'm nothing but your late night
But as long as I have your gaze in unfulfilled moments
My heart can be full just for a split second.

I'm standing right in front of your eyes
But you couldn't be more oblivious.

I've spent a whole life experiencing unrequited love for you,
I'll wait as long as I can
But the nights you're heart burns for her
Mine is left with a permanent crack
With the fear of never loving another heart
that beats the same way back.

The Way You Passed Through

We made a promise to each other the day we met
That as long as I stood here
And you were there
We would never have to feel abandoned.

But as much as hope and trust can do,
You stomped all over that, damaging
Any bit of trust I could have summoned left.

And it hurts to watch you attach yourself to someone else
Because the one person who I thought would make me whole
Couldn't wait for any time that existed without me.

Puppet Love

I think if I could
I'd camp a home in you.

Sometimes when I get so sick of my own thoughts
I think about what you'd think,
You were always better at thinking things,
I was just always irrational and manic.

Maybe I wish I was you,
Or maybe I wish I didn't have to think so much.

From the day I met you had this sort of thing that I found fascinating,
You couldn't believe it when I told you that
But you had an effortlessly complex personality,
Like you weren't even trying hard to be interesting,
You just were.

I just wanted someone to care about what I'd have to say
And for a little while that was you and likewise I did
The same for you.

And so
I sat there every day waiting till you gave me the next page of you

But you stopped giving them one day,
And you found someone who you thought was cool,
And gave your pages to them.

Because I guess in your head
I was just a passing through,
But to me I thought with you I reached the finish line
And I guess now I'm just slowly losing whatever companionship race we're all stuck in.

So now I imagine I'm a drifter and everyone can walk right through me,
Just like you did,
Because you proved that no matter how deeply affections can feel
I'm just a thinker and you were always a do-er.

Speechless

Now you've gone away,
Just because I could never find the right words to say,
But if you just looked a little further
And at least made an effort
You would see
I needn't have said much,
Because everything I felt went beyond any word
That I could string together to say out loud.

From the one you'll forget

If you ever asked me what it was like to be your second choice,
Well I'd simply say
It comes as easy as breathing.

It wasn't ever a position my mind never expected,
I stepped in line the minute you had decided
For it was already labelled for me,
I was just the girl you meet before you met her.

My brain knew how to walk away giving me some piece of mind,
It was comforting
But crushing,
Knowing I'd never disappoint you by being myself,
But destroying in the way my heart couldn't take you loving someone else.

I wasn't going to try and maybe that's what separates me every time,
Cause in my lovesick head I'd hoped someone wanted to be with me so bad that there was never going to be
Another choice.

Mismatched

Everything reminds me of you,
The octaves of someone's voice
To the reactions of bodies that are moving around.

You were made for me
But I wasn't made for you,
I'd probably do anything for us to talk again
But when I re-read the signs we spoke less and less as the days went by.

Maybe it was all inevitable,
You leaving,
me watching you go.

I used to feel comforted in the fact that when you went far,
You were never out of reached for too long,
But I never understood why we always needed so much space,
Why couldn't we merely just be.

You liked my stories,
And I liked the way you explained ideas,
So why couldn't that be enough?

But a lot of the times I was too blind to see how wrong I

must have been,
For if you were an early morning
I was a miserable night.

Wasted

You drink me up
Until you've taken me whole,
But as long as I exist in some part of your life
It doesn't matter how much of me you take and take.

Sometimes you take so much I can't breathe without you,
I fell in love with you under the trees and kissed your tears free,
You tore me apart night after night as nothing but a mistress,
Because to you that's the only way you'll ever see me.

The thing about you

I knew you never liked me
like that,
I wasn't ever even sure if I
Liked you liked that.

All I knew is that if you talked to me
It would all be okay
Just for a little while.

Until you would mention the one you did like
Like that,
And as my heart sunk a little deeper,
I couldn't differ if the feeling of you,
Was just something I was so desperately trying to sense
Or hoping that I could relate to the songs that lap around in
my head.

But it's been a while
And I'm still not even sure now
If I like you
like that.

All I ever think about is how I can cut you out,
Because of the pain you bring me every time you say
something lovely

And the way you talk about another girl's beauty.

I wish I knew what you thought about me
But my head tells me you only feel pity,
And so as long as we're friends
I'll cluster with confusion
And lack sleep
Wondering if I'll ever be happy.

But somehow whenever we're lost in exchange
I find myself thanking the universe
For bringing you to me.

Keep the lights off

What's the points of turning the lights on when we're never really seeing the truth?
The truth being you only ever saw me for the curve of weight I held when the light flickered on
But recoiled away when any moment turned acute.

You never really saw what was there in the dark either,
So
The lights couldn't save your awareness
Or your infatuation with strangers
And neither could the love that I enveloped you down into.

The girls you gaze at

I wish I could be gazed upon,
The type to cast an everlasting stare of eyes that spill every gentle expression into one look.

I watch others get gazed upon,
Staring in the background in lost hope that I'll ever be the type
To have such beauty to trigger such softness towards its beholder.

I remind myself in the mirror
And tell it to my ego every day
That no matter how pretty I feel
I'll never be the one that could gush a crowd.

I'm always trying to change
Because there seems to be a hole inside me that says
Maybe if I change this
Someone will notice and I won't have to fear I am invisible to the girls that are gazed at.

Just friends

Every day I spend my time looking at you through my flushed-out cheeks and hooded lids,
Sometimes you make me feel like the luckiest and unluckiest person alive at times.

Lucky in the way I can't believe I get to know you
But unlucky in the way that you've broken my heart a million times
And yet you have the faintest idea.

I'm just a puppy to your every move,
Sometimes I think I must snap out of this as your intentions are platonic and mine are selfishly romantic
But every-time I try your face reminds we why should I even try?

Maybe I must leave you,
Because as much as I want to be there for your every waking call
It gets hard for me to open my eyes,
When I've spent the night stuck in a parallel
That a you and I is something,
Something different to the painful realisation that I'm just your companion.

Another life

What if in another lifetime
We exist in all the ways we couldn't right now?
What if in another life kissing you is as normal as breathing
and the way we feel for each other is a simple confession
One of which we always knew fragments of.

Maybe in another life
You loved me back
To the way I loved you,
I wouldn't have to hope someone took care of you
Because I'd be there wrapping you up in my arms.

But as much as I scream, what if?
What if?
What if?
I can't help but burst at the fact that it will never be in this lifetime,
Only in the daydreams that tease me with what could have been.

In this lifetime I'll hug you with a pat,
Become an audience member to the stories of your loves from the past,
Where I'll complain about how imperfect they are for you
Because really

I'll never say how much happier you could be if only you let me in
And pushed the bad ones out.

One day you'll even get married and I'll watch you with tears in my eyes over how unfair it was
That you never chose me.

You see me as nothing

'Why can't you let me have this?'
I begged to understand you,
When did all of my achievements belong to you and become
incomparable to all the ways
You say you succeed?

You never gave me an answer
And mostly likely just punched a wall and called it a day.

You practically knew nothing about me but always expected
me to be over the moon at your next accomplishment that
came.

I'm so sick of faking happiness for you
Because just one time I wish you would ask
'How was your day?'

Alone for the century

Why aren't I effortlessly desirable?

I ache at nights
Sitting alone drowning in the facts of how I am not anybody's something,
And I haven't ever been.

Must I have to change completely for someone to feel anything?

I'm in a constant hidden state of vulnerability
With eyes that stare out begging for someone to love me.

I often claim to love the personal time,
But I want to feel giddy
And I want someone to feel that type of way about me.

I want to be looked at like I was the reason beautiful things occur,
And I want to be thought about in only the purest of forms that would make something think
That soulmates truly exist and that I
Was theirs for the taking.

The way I lost you

I don't blame you for the way you left,
I was a sad sap and you were anything but that.

On occasions though,
We were wonderful
And we were something worth missing.

For moments at a time all the beautiful parts of us got sewed together like a songwriter forming lyrics.

Except we never even got to verse two because I couldn't give myself completely to you,
And while I thought we meant more than the activities people consumed past bedtimes
You were only looking for a body to use and eventually give up on.

One sided

I don't know how I made you bored,
It came as such a shock when you admitted that whatever routine we become in a habit of
Was no longer anything you wished to continue.

How did I miss your disgusted looks?
Was it because mine were only filled with adoration?
For everyday with you I found completely captivating.

I think it's because I could get amused at the simplest of things,
But when you muttered that I dimmed your light down
Well that was the first time my heart broke completely in half.

Used

Say that you want me just for once,
Just let me pretend that I'm not in pure agony every day
when you kiss her instead of me.

Let my mind believe that I was finally good enough outside
of someone's brain that wasn't mine,
Bring a moment to me where we do and say the things
That aren't just repetitive daydreams in my head.

Please I beg you why,
Why not me?

Why do you love her so easily and throw me aside
As if you didn't even have to think about it?
Because you thought I should have known that you would
only want me as what you said was just a 'good time'.

Apparently good times were done when she finally caved
and wanted you back,
So now we don't even talk because why would we?

You just committed the nightmare I pleaded not to happen,
And without effort
It made you feel nothing.

Afraid of feelings

I wish I wasn't scared to tell you what you actually mean to me,
I wish I didn't have to hide behind secrecy.

I wish that I didn't feel so scattered just by your name,
And more importantly I just wished you felt the same.

Only you

I stood there trying to dry the tears on my face as quickly as they came,
Why didn't you wait for me,
Please tell me,
Why didn't you wait?

Am I supposed to forget and let you move on?

You're even holding someone new
And they look nothing like me so I guess your type must have changed.

I wanted to grow old with you,
Planned everything, catered to you
Waited and I pined,
Did everything you're supposed to,
Watched the clock tick by.

But while my time was passing with thoughts of you,
Yours was filled with another stranger and how to leave me without making a scene.

Now I must walk away but a part of me remains here unchanged,
And that's that you're in my head and I can't get you out,

Except
It used to make me smile
But now it's just awfully painful.

When I arrived,
I was a girl in love growing impatient for your return,
But I leave here destroyed from only you,
Only ever you.

Not picked

I'm not quite sure why you tease me and act as if
Nothing went wrong,
You talk to me so normally as if you didn't just not choose me.

Maybe I was too casual
And you underestimated how badly I had fallen for you
But the decision you made was clear.

That it was never going to be me,
You were always going to pick her,
The two of you were soulmates and I was just a disturbance.

You're not real

As we danced across my bedroom floor
Skin to skin
My eyes fluttered open
And I was reminded of something
That had never been.

Tell me the truth

I stared at your lips telling a story
I wondered which parts were true
And what parts you had threaded through.

The problem is,
I no longer can tell the difference
And for once
I just wanted you tell me something real.

Songs I used to play

A certain song used to remind me of you
But now I just sit and let it play.

It used to make me scream and describe everything I couldn't say,
Now it's background noise and makes me pity how naïve I must have been,
For you were just the only guy that would acknowledge that I exist.

My feelings for you faded over time,
For I think I must have had the wrong idea about you for many nights.

When we hadn't talked for months, I didn't miss you
And by your lack of response, I'd say you thought the same,
I would say you betrayed me but maybe that's exaggerating words we never said.

It's sad because I thought you were the only one that understood me
And for a little while I needed that
But I think now that you were only trying to fix my negative qualities
For it seemed that you had a bit of saviour complex with

every girl you met.

Nothing could have enraged me more than when I realised that,
Because you left me just as easy as the way you entered my life
And it's funny because I hated you at first,
And I wish I still did
But I guess people come and go and you were only meant to be there
For a short while.

The ones

You wanted them to be the ones who loved you inside and out,
The ones who would never think to plan something without you being there.

But they were the ones
And the past people were also the ones,
So
You hid away in a bedroom soaked through with your tears asking yourself
Why did I always pick the bad ones?

Why did you always pick the ones that never stayed,
The ones that pretended to know you
But couldn't possibly be more wrong,
The ones that faked empathy and only wanted to be around you for insignificant time.

This was always your cycle and it would surely come again,
But for now
You're alone like most of your hours
Until the next ones come again and you get caught up in the excitement that follows from new attachments,
Just to be disappointed that another person didn't end up in your corner.

Burn me

You created something big in me,
A potential I had never felt I was deserving of
But you grew distasteful of it and tried to crush that empowerment I had never felt.

So,
I realised
no matter how great I could become,
It was only alright if it didn't outshine whatever light you thought you had.

What a time

I missed the time where I was all yours,
Now I don't know how to go on
Because your touch was the only thing that got me through anything
And now I lay still waiting for any sort of intimacy.

I thought you wanted me forever,
You treated me like your endgame and told others how undeniably in love you were with me
But that was mere a phase and now a lifetime exists where you have moved on
And I'm still standing here.

I wished you'd told me something real
Something like how you never really loved me,
But you never did,
You just came into my life one day to sweep me into a dream and show me how good
Things could have been,
Just to leave me in a nightmare without any kind of feeling.

Irreversibly yours

To be irreversibly yours
Meant to live in a world I had everything I could have asked for.

To be the one you chose immediately
In a way only my most favourite daydreams thought of,
Well, I'd give anything for that.

Anything for a second glance
Or a moment of longing,
I'd give it all to feel everything with you,
To know what it feels like to be the one that you adore.

Our love is one-sided
But nevertheless beautiful,
For you my dearest
I'd rather experience this feeling of never receiving anything back
than to live without knowing
What it feels like to fall for someone like you.

I may not be content always,
Especially on the nights where your lack of presence speaks volumes,
But at least I can say I fell in love with the most wonderful person I had the luck of meeting.

To be yours

Had you said I was the one,
I would have come undone,
To be your one meant I was exactly who I wanted to be.

All I ever wanted from you was for you to kiss me like I've never been kissed,
Hold me like I've never been held,
Stay here because you wouldn't want to be anywhere else
And tell me things that you've always wanted to share.

One hundred times

For the hundred times I didn't know my feelings,
I know them now.
For the hundred times I never saw you,
You're all I see now.

For all the hundred times you saw me,
You've finally given up now.
For the hundred times you hid your feelings,
They have now slid away from you.

All I want is to take back time,
Before I missed my chance,
So I could call you mine.

Eyes that hate

Your eyes seem to hate me,
And maybe mine do too,
But I don't think our hatred is built on the same reasons,
It never usually is.

Your eyes are filled with daggers,
Mine covered with shields,
An aimless attempt to cover how much I wish you didn't look at me like that.

You've ruined me

Eat me alive, that's all you do anyway,
Steal everything that's mine,
It wouldn't change a thing.

Curse me forever,
You've already done it to my heart plenty of times,
Ruin my body,
It doesn't matter, you've already ruined it for anyone else.

If you could do anything
Reverse everything
Just so that I could bare a day and not have to think about all the things you've done to me.

Contactless digital strangers

I'm not sure if you watch my life through pictures,
If you did, I'd never know,
You just leave an empty like.

The way you left had me stepping through holes,
My feet drowning in all the gaps you put between us.

I struggled to find an answer to why whatever we were
could just turn into us being
Contactless digital strangers,
But you always left me with more questions than answers,
Even when we were tangled up in hours of communication.

Colour me in you

It's different with you,
I know people tend to say that a lot,
But I now understand what those people mean.

Everything you do I'm endlessly aware of,
Because if you ever said anything nice to me it could touch me forever,
More than any other praise another could mutter.
It's scary to admit that,
That no one else could ever have that effect on me.

I'm painted yours
But you haven't even picked up a brush,
Colour me in,
Make me forget what it was like when I was not be in your orbit,
Tell me everything you're feeling is different
Because it's with me.

Look at me like you never want to look at anything else,
Because I've only ever wanted to be in your spotlight,
Just for once in your life try to imagine me as something more,
And tell me you loved it
Because it hurts more as the days go by where you haven't.

Not a chosen one

What happens when some of us don't get picked?
Do we learn to accept there is no one is coming for us
Or continue to lose hope day by day
When we don't meet the perfect one?

I wanted to be chosen for once,
Chosen like it was the simplest choice for someone,
Singled out on a gloomy day
Instead of a background pair of a random set of legs.

Against all odds,
I just wanted to feel what it was like to be wanted,
To not have to swallow down feelings because I already
knew the only possible outcome.

At the end of the day,
There is no one knocking at my door
And the only romances I speak of are the ones I read of,
There are no arms to wrap around me in the darkest hours
of the night,
Nobody that cares on the evenings I can't sleep.

To the people that aren't wanted,
It's a rough road to take,
For you start to doubt why no one else can see the things

inside you,
Or why not one person wanted all the things you had to offer.

Your love in seasons

When we first met you loved certain things about me
That you would soon hate,
You cherished my voice and the simple things I did
That I was convinced no one noticed.

For the first few months back in summer
You said I was exciting
And that you'd die just to touch me,
Summer left us happy,
It left my parents proud.
Then came fall,
I thought I had it all,
You in my bed spending practically every night connecting deeper,
The leaves were falling
And so was I,
So very deeply and all for you.

Winter was next
And you were preoccupied,
I gave you space but that meant I would wait days
Before you stopped by,
You left me cold
And confused as my world started freezing over.

Spring came crashing down
And so did you,
Me a victim to your words and hands.
As the flowers were blooming I sat and spaced out
Thinking of how much I missed summer
Where I was who you wanted me to be.

My hatred for Tuesday

We casually said goodbye
Like it was just another Tuesday,
That was it.
Nothing else of us now remained,
You were my first everything and now just someone that I would soon miss.

I always hated Tuesdays,
They felt severely underwhelming,
We could have departed on a Wednesday but alas we couldn't wait another day,
I despised how our final words fell under a day with this particular name,
Because we were everything
But our last memory now resides underneath a pile of things that happen on a Tuesday.

The thing wrong with it is that Tuesday doesn't know how on Friday we went on our first date,
Tuesday will never experience what it felt like the first time I became yours
Or the secret smiles we gifted each other that swelled our cheeks into a blushing mess,
Tuesday will only know the love we threw away
And that's why I hated Tuesdays.

What do you do when there's no one calling your name?

Mindless chatter was all it was,
My voice grew sick of asking the same questions
And receiving boring confirmations
From people I had met a hundred times before.

The looking was exhausting
And I just wanted a moment,
It didn't matter if it was in a coffee shop
Or if someone ran into me on the side of a street.

My time was simply running out and so was my hope
That I would ever find someone that was
Meant for me.

There was no one to call
When my head became too much
And my insides started to scream.

There was only me,
It was how it always came to be,
But just for an hour I wish there was someone,
Just have a little company.

Bitter watcher

I often saw couples walking by,
The people themselves were none of my business
But I couldn't help but grow bitter
Over how lovely it seemed to be that grossly in love in for everyone to see.

I guess when you've never been with someone
You start telling people you like to be alone,
Even when all you've ever dreamed of was having a person there.

I went through so many failed attempts at intimacy
And it made me wonder why people only wanted me when I was fourteen.

A time when we were meant to be

There was a time when all I had was you on my mind,
I thought about everything I wanted to do with you,
Big dreams I planned for us to have.

When we grew older,
I watched you do those things alongside someone else,
I'd have died just to experience what that felt like,
But I just watched from distance and thought whoever you chose
Must have been the luckiest girl.

I couldn't ever imagine doing those things with someone who wasn't you,
It wouldn't be worth it
And I couldn't bare that,
So I let those dreams die
Because if it wasn't with you
I couldn't bring myself to do it with anyone again.

For the short time I had you,
My life felt more than complete,
Now you've given that sense of belonging to another
And I wonder if the thought of my name pains you,
Or is just a fleeting thought had with no meaning
And rather you just remembering who you were before you met her.

Fall asleep without me

How do you fall asleep
When you mean nothing to me?

Do you constantly roll at night wishing that I could have held on tighter to you
Or do you thank whatever is out there that we're no longer tied together?

I could never read your emotions
And you always failed to tell me how exactly you felt,
It was a confusing time to say the least
But it pains me to know
That I cry and pine over someone who never had a single thought about me.

Stuck on you

You were constantly confusing,
Every day you shifted into a different personality,
The way I realised I felt more for you
I begged my feelings to hide safely in my brain.

You were always giving me mixed signals,
Leaving me feeling utterly useless one minute
And then teasing me till my face went crimson.

I couldn't tell if it was all one sided
And you were like that with just about anyone
But you fell for different types of people which was obvious to see.

I would never tell you what you do to me,
There was no need to rush,
And I think all it was
Was a stupid crush,
Even though some nights it left me restless and with burning jealousy.

Directed by you

You own all my misery,
I think your awareness of that made you grow with satisfaction,
Knowing that you were capable of that much destruction.

I tried to hide my vulnerability to you for as long as I could,
But the day it was found,
Your eyes turned dark and you latched onto it
And discovered every way you could manipulate me.

We became a losing battle,
And I was losing myself deeply,
You made me go silent to a point
Where I would sit there and not notice how many days went by.

There was no love anymore,
There was only control
And now I was just a person you directed
No longer capable of my own thoughts.

The monster you created in me

Look what you've done to me,
I've become the crazy you've always proclaimed I was,
My hair is torn
And my eyes are blown.

So good job,
You've finally won,
I stepped into the role of being the monster
That you titled me to anyone who would care.

Everyone hates me
Because you've threatened anyone that comes in my radius
And now I'm alone just like you wanted,
My life has been ruined and human kind seems to be lacking in any sort of decency.

I watched you move on,
Not even a day later
And all I'm left to say is that
I hope you don't put anyone through the same cruelty.

Fragile pieces

I could somehow feel everything falling apart,
There was heart break in the air,
And fragile people that would collapse any second
Everywhere.

How do we put things back together
And what still remains?
When will we find peace
If it's only ever taken away?

We were all uncompleted puzzle pieces that no one bothered to shape,
Our edges were unmatchable.
So
alone we stayed,
Begging for help without ever making a sound,
Hoping someone could tell
That we had no faith in this life.

How does it feel?

How does it feel to know that you left
And left someone without feeling anything
But recognising that what you did would destroy me?

You said that we never felt right,
I tried to look back at everything to understand what made you think that,
But I guess while I was blinded by how much I adored you
It was not clear to me that your walls were still built high.

You called me a child and that I was ignorant to real life
Which made me cry because
Why weren't we real
And what did you hide?

You leaving made me question everything,
My reality and why I never saw the red signs
And the obvious looks of disgust that you threw
That were not done jokingly.

Eager to please your eyes

You called me an attention seeker most of the time,
If I had never heard of my name before
I would have mistaken it for that
With the amount of times you claimed it over me.

But I wasn't like that with anyone else,
I was just so starved of your attention,
It was like an antidote that you never gave out,
You always muttered on about my stupidity
Like I wasn't worthy to take up any of your vision.

Clueless I was,
To whether you even saw me as a friend
Or someone that you didn't completely dislike,
Because there wasn't an instance that I could recall
Where you directly spoke
A compliment towards my oblivious self.

Dedicated

You had destroyed me in every type of way
And yet here I foolishly was,
Hoping you'd still be devoted to me,
I had nothing if I didn't have you,
My only source of excitement came from the days we were together,
Every word you said had me clinging to a couch
Watching every syllable you said fall out.

It was magical the way you did things
And even when you crushed me in the palm of your hand,
For some reason I thought it was still better than if you if you gave me nothing.

Useless girl

Every part of my body I eagerly handed to you,
Your love came with a cost
And I was willing to give you every payment
Even if it took my sanity.

But on lonely nights when I would wander the streets
And look at people whose love came for free,
I wished that you would look at me like you couldn't bare
time without me,
Instead of the eyes I was always met with
That were laced with the question
Of when I would next give in.

It was better being with you than alone,
Because no one else touched me before we met
So I thought maybe this was my love story
And this was all I'd ever get.

No one looked at me without asking for a price to be made,
Which made me question if I was just one of those people
That would get tossed around like an unwanted toy.
I longed for someone to answer that for me
So that I didn't have hope that someone might come into my
life
And make me forget every way I had been bruised.

Mass manipulator

You had everything,
So why did you feel the need to take more?
What were you so hungry for?
To a point where nothing was ever enough.

There was nothing you did for anyone,
All you did was seek more people
That were willing to give you the things you thought you
were so starving for.

For a while you had me tricked,
On the matter that you were worth all the finer things I
could offer,
But you were nothing,
Complete garbage,
A mass manipulator
Hiding behind smiles and affectionate touches.

Temporary friendship

We never had a stagnant friendship,
Which is why it made me mad that you thought
Talking to me was like entering a door,
And then keeping it shut for weeks.

I was always labelled as temporary in your box of items,
You never really cared about our deep conversations,
To you I was just another one of your victims
Placed in the bin to rot
Just like the others until you decided to recycle us
And wear us out again.

You never kept anyone forever,
But you also had the ability to make a girl forgive you with the simplest touch of your hand,
I hated being another one of your projects,
Just something you thought you could fix.

The only thing I wanted was for you to properly notice me
Through and through,
And adore that memory full heartedly,
But you only ever moved on and traced your heart into girls that didn't realise
What awaited them.

Everyone forgot

On the corner of the street,
There were still parts of me ghosted through the pavement,
Every place you left me
I remained
Collecting in old remnants,
Staring at the clouded air
Wondering when you would pick me up.

You moved on and started fresh in a new biosphere
That was filled with different city lights,
But I was stuck in this horrible world,
Only filled with past memories,
Waiting for anyone to remember who they lost
And run to save me.

If I changed, would you remember where I last stood?
Maybe realise you couldn't stay away for another day
Or was I out of match?
Did we no longer have anything in common
Besides the time we spent together?

I was scared you would never come back,
But I stayed anyway,
Hoping that one day you would free me from the time
You froze me into.

Holes in my arteries

I ached with want to be placed with someone,
There was an immense painful hole stuck in my arteries,
Growing and swelling impossibly large,
Each day that I continued to go unnoticed
And unmatched to anyone that orbited my world.

My soul was forced to be fiercely independent
While my head was trying to cling onto a daydream,
I thought by now I would have a story to tell
But I was doomed with the traits I had been given
That acted as a repellent to all the things I wanted.

Time made me hostile
And I convinced myself that it would be awful to have these obligations
Even though I was just lying through my teeth,
Acting like I despised romantic connections
When it was the one thing I ached for the most on this earth.

Tell me we're something more

What if we acted differently to what we're used to,
Maybe it would be nice to treat each other like we cared
Rather than looking past one another as if we were strangers,
Your eyes can be so cold and cruel
And it hurt that you could so easily pretend I meant nothing to you.

It was possible that that was true,
Maybe I was just skin for your use
But sometimes when your touch becomes a gentle graze
I like to imagine that you want all of me,
Not just in your free time.

Envy.
Was what I felt for whoever finally broke you down
Because I just wanted to know what it felt like
To be in your arms,
In a way that was filled with pure warmth,
Instead of the dirty hands you put on me
Telling me that I am nothing but a body
Incapable of having thoughts.

Tear me down

Every chance we got to exchange words,
I was left feeling overly pathetic,
You just had this power over me to make me feel as if
Any mumble I managed to make
Was a waste of energy
And a tragedy to your eyes.

How is it that you make me beg for a slither of confirmation
Just to know that you even slightly enjoyed my company,
You would never give in to being vulnerable,
So I just kept my mouth shut,
Let you do all the talking so that you wouldn't abandon me.

The end

Why did we have to have a sad ending?
Was it always to be destined that one of us would end
In pure agony
And if that was the case was everyone aware
That it was going to be me?

The events of the death of us
Was a doomsday,
And brutally done without a care.
I asked you to be careful with how you killed me
But you ignored my requests and stomped over every sensitive artery
That was filled with the parts I thought you liked.

You turned silent
And it was as if you had let go of a dead weight,
I never felt as insignificant as I did on that day,
Paralysed on the floor while your eyes flashed with
something I had never been aware of.

New Year's Eve

The last day of the year used to be exciting,
It felt like entering a new era,
Each one worth having,
But now there was no point
And all I did was go to sleep
Just to wake up the next day writing the end of my dates
with a different number.

Maybe it's the repetition as I get older
That's slowing it down
Having not a single person to celebrate with
As the fireworks are sounding loud,
It just starts to feel like one long moment
Without an ending,
Making it even more tiresome every time I blink
And am brought back to life.

All I can do is sigh and try not to be cynical
Because as much as I try to be optimistic
Dejection and angst are the only things passing my mind.

Getaway guy

You had told me to let you go,
It was your escape route,
That you had planned months ago.
Now I sit in a bed that is soaked,
Clutching picture frames wondering when you decided to slice this tangible thing we had
Into shreds.

If your smile had given away any insinuations
I still could have never seen it coming,
How can I let you go
When you were the best thing that had happened to me?

When did our timeline rearrange to make me go from living in your presence
To waving last goodbyes
And staring at photos that showed a story of the past.

Be the one to stay

Objects around us were flying out of place,
We were no longer in control of the things
Our hands desperately once contained in our possessions,
You couldn't touch me,
Our bodies were too far apart,
So you stopped trying and launched yourself into the unknown.

I was left unaccompanied, forced to fight through objects that contained
Too much impact,
Why weren't you there to help?
Was the distance not guaranteed and that terrified you too much so
That you let the space between us carry you to someone else.

Now I'm struggling in a losing battle,
Giving up on future hope that there might be a person out there
Capable of embracing the changes that come in heats.

Ripped

You set me free even when you knew
I only wanted to be held in your captivity,
Our final doings were said under a cluster of confusion,
Yours were sad goodbyes,
And mine were begs that you'd take it all back.

Was there anything I could have done to show you I was
ready for this,
There was nothing to fix
Except now I knew what it felt like to experience bliss,
But never fully so
Because before I got the chance you discarded your feelings.

The last sentence you spoke to me
Were words along the lines of how I needed to find myself,
I was alone for most of life so all I ever could do was that
Self-awareness was not something that I found to be
complicated,
My body knew who I was
But it wasn't good enough.

Falling

Water drops down,
Staining my face,
Changing the temperature of where your hands last fell,
Things are broken on the ground
And you've told me you never loved me.

There's nothing I can do to hold the water up,
My face is drowning,
And my eyes are too blurry to notice anything,
Your verses would never be shared with mine again,
We would have no future memories,
It was all done.
Closing time had appeared and you had sentenced me to tragedy.

Ornaments that spoke volumes of us
Were shattered on my ground,
No longer a reminder of a painful association,
Just broken glass that would only exist now in wastelands.

Taken

I would have taken anyone that decided to have me,
But why did it have to be you?
You burned me and swept me away in a fire,
My skin fell from the flames and my eyes still remembered the way we started.

It was a cliché story of our eyes meeting,
The flowers and homemade dinners,
Somehow along the way of too many make-outs and tiring conversations,
Your flowers started dying
And you tried to poison me.

Do you remember how you used to feel when we first met?
Perhaps it was all lies
Concealed through false sincerity,
But you told me that I took your breath away,
Which is ironic since now you're taking mine.

I find it unmanageable now,
To believe you ever spoke such kind words once before
Since our days are usually spent
Filled with venomous attacks,
Your spit flying out as you tell me how worthless I am.

Decomposing till I am seen

For so long I had only been wanted
In a way that was purely based on seamless threads,
No one knew me but some people used to like the idea of me,
Enough so that they thought I could be their trophy.

Now no one bothers to look at me,
Because I've lost my shine
And no one wants a rusty trophy.

The old idea of me has faded,
So I've become nothing.
Hidden in the shadows where all that hasn't been claimed
Rots away.

I wouldn't say I missed being seen through the lens of boys that were disingenuous,
But I begged that someone would wipe my rust clean
And realise that I can be new again.

Wounds

Don't stand so close
When you choose to not be near.
Let me heal the wounds you sliced
Instead of being indecisive on whether you'll have me.

You always wait for me to make a move
So that there's never a chance of you being rejected,
But I've given up on our skin touching
And our lips brushing
Because I can't wait in line for you to barely even try.

Cut up

Missing you like it's the only thing I know
Is something that has shaped my entire being,
Life is shallow when my body is without your depth
But you have let me drown and forget what having you is like.

Take me in completely,
Stop requiring me in doses
Because it seems unfair that I only crave the whole of you
Just to be met with a quarter of our affair back.

Human Connection

Sing me to sleep

She felt as if she could just be with him,
They could just merely exist together and that was always enough,
She loved him more than one could ever love a person,
It tore her apart
But there wasn't ever a time she spent without loving him.

They only ever loved each other in silence,
Two hearts that longed for each other but were too scared to live without the other,
She knew it meant she was destined a painful life with a hopeless, broken heart, but it was
Worth it rather than never living a life in his shape.

So that was what she did,
She watched him sleep next to other people
And he watched her.

What they both didn't know is while they were sharing beds with strangers
Their hearts longed and ached for the same thing,
It seemed impossible for the other to comprehend losing each other,
That the only way they could be with each other the way they wanted

Was in their dreams.

While it was okay for a while it began to eat them alive,
They sneaked glances at one another while the other wasn't looking and cried themselves to sleep,
They married different people and learned to accept living with a broken heart.

One day it became too much for him
And he couldn't possibly bare to live in a world where he wasn't loved by the person who tears his heart open.
The only girl who made him feel alive and completely whole with just a simple touch.
So
He swallowed what he could, anything to not feel the complete emptiness and heartache he had felt for twenty years.

She had stopped by to see him and it felt as if the world was playing her movements in slow motion,
This twist of events had to be some sick joke.
Before she saw him, there was a note.
Of course
There was a note,
Its white shade with so many words scribbled on the pages,
It titled her as his only love,
His person,
The only woman he could possibly ever love.

The tears never stopped streaming, she ran over to him,
Cradled his near-death body

All she wanted was more time,
But time was not on their side,
Not now,
it wasn't ever.

They always loved each-other incomparably
But were never ones to take a chance,
That hurt her deep inside as he took his last breath.

Ugly Moon

We stand here, our feet crushing the grass beneath us. Things have changed but we're just looking at the trees sway to do anything but accept that. I've changed, I have different passions and you feel as if this version of me is not the one you fell in love with. The sun reflects onto your eyes and makes them that honey brown I always loved, except those eyes are filled with secrets I don't know. Time will make us realise we don't feel the same about another but moving on hurts. We've said words we can't take back; our love isn't something to be admired, but it once was the most enchanting thing I had ever experienced. The old us was something I would have dreamed endless nights about, but now you're you, and I have no idea who that is. I didn't realise I could feel so deeply and complex about a person that it shattered me when we did what we did. All that love completely ruined, what once could be compared to flowers blooming turned into the feeling you get when dirt is stuck on your feet. Maybe nothing is wrong, maybe we're just making this up because what we had was too perfect for too long and we couldn't fathom that. My hair has changed to that shade you hate, and my skin looms paler by the second. We haven't said everything we need to, our hearts begging us for one more moment until they don't have to depart. I knew we would grow older but I'd always say no matter who you are I'd endlessly love you, but clearly as our feet ache my head wants to spit you out. You were as beautiful and enchanting as the moon when we first met, but now with the things you have done, your soul has turned as ugly as ever. We leave as broken, our heart chains that were in one piece broken on the dirt of the place we last stood together.

Suddenly All I See Is You

I wished for a lot of things,
You were not one of them.

But the day that you came,
I found myself wondering
How I could have wished for anything else.

We were intertwined

"So, I love you," you said, with no question laced behind it, only fearless aspiration. It took me by the surprise at how certain you sounded, so I asked you again. Without hesitation you repeated yourself, "So I love you." I couldn't believe my ears; I was existing in a world with another person that actually saw me for who I am. Your eyes blinked but patently waited for only you knew what kind of love I had only ever experienced, but with you it was so very different, for everything with you was different.
I was a flowing tune when I was with you, so I mustered as much certainty my voice could handle and replied, "Of course I love you too, how could I not?" That was all it took for us to finally connect and be with each other in a way that was an unspoken bond there all along. The pupils of your eyes widened as if what I said was completely shock worthy which was something utterly implausible in my brain for you were the most beautiful entity my soul had ever aligned with. We grimaced in anticipation for what came next, but I didn't need to wait no further because at last, you took me in your arms and that was everything and everything I could ever need.

Soulmates

Our feet are jumping through fields,
We've never felt so free,
Being with you sets my soul into a million flames.

You warm my skin
And hold my heart in your hand.

I can't think of time that lapped without you,
You're all I see,
I don't have to be afraid anymore.
As long as you're here breathing with me
My soul will never have to hurt again.

Today is just one of the many days of forever with you,
We don't have to be lonely ever again,
Living a life in your shape,
An everlasting paradise.

Almost

We lay here searching for something,
Asking the midnight sky to bless us with something we can understand.
I'm trying to understand you
And you're trying to understand me.

The air feels crisp,
My mind pretending that we could have this moment romantically.

You inch closer to me,
And as cliché as can be,
My heart skips a beat.

When our gaze falls upon eyes that lay too close
We search for clarity in one and other,
Begging the other to admit their underlying love
But in the spur of the moment one of us looks away.

Another moment hidden in the almost.

Kids in Heat

We were chasing the edge of the world,
Igniting each other on fire with excitement that we craved from the world.

There wasn't anything we couldn't do,
All I needed was to look in your eyes and that was all the comfort I would ever need.

We don't have much,
But it never mattered because being with you was like exploring something deep inside myself
Every day.

Discovering you as a person inside and out has been the greatest gift this life has ever given me.

We knew how we felt for each other before we even knew what love was,
It was just sitting there this whole time waiting for us to find out what to call it.

I didn't need to play some guessing game on whether or not you felt the same,
It was just common knowledge there all along,
Because we were something that only happens in fantasy.

Crooked Smiles

If I had to pick a memory of you,
It would be this one,
You sat there with the most blinding smile I'd ever seen,
In that moment you were the happiest you'd ever been.

With the corners of your smile crooked in a way you usually
would be insecure of,
But behold was my favourite part of you,
And seeing that fixed every crack of ugly I had in me.

Don't leave

Being with you was like taking a breath of fresh air,
Usually, I was a person filled with dread,
But you awoke something in me that I didn't know was still there.

So,
I wish this moment and moments with you to last till forever,
Because I'm afraid my dear
That if we spend any waking minute afar
I'll simply crumble apart.

Your words

I hate the words that spew from my lips,
The random absurdity that listeners would dismiss.

If I ever looked to you,
You'd know what I always wanted to say.

I wanted to be more than the ramble of diction that came out of my mouth,
And you saw me for exactly that.

You saw me for my movements,
My actions,
My dreams and aspirations.

Maybe my love for you was selfish
But you just had a flawless perception of seeing things for what they are,
And that just made me want to drown myself in you and see what I was like from the other side.

Loved by a Narcissist

Sometimes I wished so badly that you would say sorry just because I was so used to shutting down to the face of a narcissist.

I always thought you were to compassionate to be one to not communicate
But as I threw myself into the early days of your affections and gave you everything
You couldn't wait to unleash your wrath of control
Which you so desperately hid in order for me to be yours.

I wish I knew if you felt bad,
I wish I didn't have to argue all the time,
Defend myself each day that goes by.

Why couldn't you let me have one thing?

Everything was yours including my body and mind and I guess I shrugged when you took that,
Because I slowly didn't care and forgot how much I once loved my own company.

Words we don't mean

How do we erase words we don't mean?

There wasn't an ounce of my body that fully believed the words that were coming out of my mouth,
So why am I saying such distasteful things out loud?

How do we stop the awful aggression of words from spilling out?

I want only to be with you so badly so
My body is subjected to the feeling of yours alone.

I wish for the look you gave me at this moment to fade into the memory of soft eyes I'm used to,
I want to curl up into your shirt and beg you to stay because I know that with one night of
Regretful words,
We'll be nothing in the morning and positively nothing could hurt me more than becoming someone
You used to know.

I can't bare the way words that keep falling out of my lips without permission,
Angry enough to stop whatever speech you're giving.

How did we get to these false accusations when we were once only made up of love declarations?

The day I saw you again

When I saw you for the first time after we detached, I couldn't clear my head nor the memories that came rushing back. How was I supposed to approach a person who had made me go through every state of emotion more intensely than I thought I was ever capable of. We always drifted towards one another for I knew you for a million years before we were together, maybe that's why it hurts so much that us talking is no longer part of my routine because we not only wrecked a relationship, but we lost one of the most beautiful friendships I had ever experienced. My eyes broke your stare first because I feared if I looked any longer my eyes would betray me and start to tear. The way we left things felt corrupt to the universe as if we entered some time dimension that was possibly the worst outcome. I couldn't even manage to portray a smile because you were the only person, I couldn't fake emotion towards, for you could see right through me. If only I was a little earlier to where I was, we wouldn't be having this exchange, but maybe I wouldn't take it back because no matter how badly our circumstances are, I need you all the way throughout this lifetime and any lifetime's past.

Last times

Let's just sit around and wait for a while,
If this is going to be the last time
We see each other
Then what's the rush?

I know you'd rather be anywhere else,
But while we sit here can't we realise all the reasons we fell in love,
Or reminisce on the start of us
Before we knew that this was how it ends?

I'm afraid you won't soak it up,
Because I'm using all this time to remember that even though not all relationships are supposed to last
We can still think of ours and think,
'For what it's worth, well we had something good.'

I hate that soon this will be my new normal and you'll only be a thing of the past,
Because I want to visit that place with you one more time,
I want to listen to our songs before we can't bear to play them,
I want to share one more laugh because only you knew what I truly found funny.

Let's revisit all the events of our past and comment on how naïve we used to be,
Even though we knew that we were very serious and it's utterly devasting that we turned out to be,
Not quite the perfect match that we once thought we could have been.

Someone that I used to know

I hate who you turned out to be
When you used to have the sweetest soul.

What ever happened to that part of you?
Did someone tear it down and you couldn't bother to build it up?

Did someone dry it all up
And you feel as if everyone is not worth whatever kind deed you could fulfil them?

I watch you grow from afar because we drifted and none of us bothered to stabilise,
The friendship of ours that was soon from ending,
But if communication was still a regular occurrence for us every day,
I would ask you how you came to be this way,
Was it just a matter of maturing
Or this just the new you?

The new you
I never saw coming.

You

I don't know how I didn't see it
But believe me it's all I see now.

Every beautiful light soaked you through and through and I saw something in you I had never seen before.

It's you,
It's always been you,
And I know that sounds cheesy
But I've never had a revelation as strong
As the one that's just washed over me now.

This night feels different
And I'm slightly afraid of what's to come,
But really I just need you in all the ways we had never bothered to explore.

Somewhere Only We Know

Things felt heavy,
Everyone was turning corrupt,
Suffocating us till we couldn't breathe,
So why don't we escape even if you have to be home before the sun comes up.

I can only rely on the space I have with you,
Because our space is precious
And it's the only place unaltered by anyone else.

Now I no longer know where I start
And you finish because you've changed my soul
With every touch you've given,
That I feel every fact we could have told anyone about us
Remains tangled beneath the veins in our skin.

I didn't want to get to attached
But with you I needn't worry about self-doubt,
I just said can we please go somewhere and pretend that no one else exists
And that every conflicting war only needs a kiss to fix.

My favourite form of love

It was quite special the way we loved each other,
The way I felt about you could make any situation bearable
And always gave me a safe haven at the end of an awfully plain day.

I never thought I would experience falling in love as I was cynical for most of my life,
But the moment you came
Any expectation or aggression I held decayed
And I knew that you were what I had unintentionally begged for,
Now all I can do is
hope that you want to stay.

Perfect

Fundamentally,
There was nothing wrong.

There was a wife and a husband
With money to spend
And a white picket fence.

Inside their heads,
Everything had completely failed.
For now
they had infidelity and hearts that were impaled.

They were high school sweethearts,
So how could such hatred bloom and tear them apart?

They started with nothing,
Worked to achieve everything.

They lie in thoughts of divorce and don't think about the
times when they were in love,
Where everything was so sweet and exhilarating.

They could leave now,
And nothing would happen
Except one heart would remain shattered
On the carpet inside of the house that lays
Daisies out the front that don't age.

The girl at the bus stop

The girl at the bus stop sat on the bench at quarter to ten nearly every day. She waited and waited, for she would sit there an hour early and watch cars go by patiently awaiting the bus's arrival, or maybe even for someone to come by. The bench was flat and uncomfortable, but the girl didn't pay it much mind as her fingers were to invested in flicking through worn out pages.

"This day feels different," she said, like she did almost every other opaque morning, and so she sat hoping for the best, hoping that something would appear outside of her daily routine. She felt someone's stare radiating through her, drawing her eyes towards it like a magnet, while her mind internally screamed at this perfect stranger. He sat next to her and the possibilities in the girl's head were scrambled as endless.

It took her by surprise when the next time she looked up, there was no to be seen, not a person nor a peep. This occurrence shouldn't have been shocking since she had maladaptive daydreams and at last, she was just alone again. Alone again on another quarter to ten morning at the bus stop, reading stories she wished would happen to her.

Seasons come and go

We grow accustomed to the fact that none of us can change
When we're the only ones keeping things the same.

We hated every season just because they either lasted too
long
Or not long enough.

Every day we got thrown into a world we could never adapt
to and tried to find stability in each other,
But the longer months passed that we hated,
We found neither comfort or love from another and became
another cycle of human connection
That wasn't worth the compensation.

Falling for people you aren't supposed to

The rain is pouring outside and we're sitting in a room uncertain of things to be. The weather is inconstant and so are we, fighting to figure out what to make of the sudden changes we have endured. I've made things this way by repeating my feelings that you never felt back, so here we sit, a broken heart and another that longs for something else. It wasn't your fault you never felt anything back, for I never expected anything I just needed the words out and for someone besides me be aware. To disappear would be better just to give this friendship some space, you never wanted this but I selfishly made things this way, so I'll watch you leave and never return because secretly I want you to finish the damage and never talk to me again, just to give my head a chance to breathe. That's what we do when we fall in love with people we aren't supposed to, they beg us to stay and we push them out.

When we aligned

I kissed and kissed and kissed you
Till my lungs gave out and you were a remedy
I desperately swallowed.

Gave into you while you glued me down,
Stuck me to your body wrapped around completely.

You held on tight
And acted polite.

The time stopped and I felt everything at once,
Every moment I missed and wanted to last,
You were there bringing me back.

We were floating on soft rugs and delving through touches
we craved every minute that passed.

We laughed and soaked up the night,
It all felt complete even the stars were aligned.

We were touch starved but only wanted to touch each other,
Every second we craved more,
We were fulfilling everything that could have been,
Confessions were spilled and candles had warmed up the night.

We were two bodies that grew together and shaped around one another,
The truths were laid out and now all that was left was a forever
With us entwined.

Your power

How could you say such things as if they don't hold so much power?

You answered,
"Because they don't, it was neither a revelation nor a declaration, it was simply the only thing I found to be true in this world."

Those words held weight,
Enough weight for the both of us
But I didn't mind if for the rest of our lives,
I was the only thing holding the both of us up.

I could carry the both of us through everything,
For as long you would have me.

Time spent with you

Sometimes when we were together
I felt like I could melt time within itself,
It didn't matter if it had only been five minutes
With you,
It felt like every clock stopped
And we were incapable of changing the way our bodies flowed.

Time with you
Meant not checking what the hour was,
It meant living and forgetting how the days roll in.

That's why I loved every moment you were with me
Because it meant a moment where the only thing I had on my mind
Was how special it was to be living a life alongside you.

Flipped for you

Things have changed,
I think to myself as I sit in this empty lobby.

The air shifted and forced us into something we weren't familiar with,
We grew into victims of uncomfortable feelings,
The way you sat in the chair across from mine
Made it easy to tell you felt the same,
You knew that we were different
But I couldn't tell if you hated it and that mere fact alone
Terrified me.

As soon as the change cast a spell upon us
I thanked it more than I had thanked anything in my life,
It made everything become so clear
And I flipped myself inside and out just in hopes you would look up and say my name,
Or tell me every feeling you've had lately that is driving you insane.

Imperfect beauties

I was always living half awake
With my eyes tinted grey,
There was nothing I bothered to see
But I wasn't always looking.

Till I saw you,
It felt like for the first time I was seeing colour.
You brought me alive
And made my lifeless body twirl around and come back to life.

We ran and ran even when there was nothing and everything to run from,
We were just running to soak up every bit of happiness that covered our atmosphere.

Now that I see the world in all shades of you,
I'm not sure what made me so blind before.
But whenever you stray far, I become afraid of the dark
Because I don't want you to forget the girl filled in grey
I want you to bring me with you
And bathe me in your yellow hue.

The only thing that made me feel anything was the way you spoke to me.

With eyes that peered into mine like they couldn't believe I was real,
I wanted to keep that in a time capsule and bottle it up,
Just so that I could prove to people one day
That I was once looked at like I meant something.

My mind is not stupid, I know for a fact I can't keep you,
The dull light I attain would only impair you more so each day,
Your radiance needed light, and I hoped whoever you chose was brighter than any star that
Shone through our universe.

The short time I had with you
Has meant more to me than I let on for most to believe,
You made me see colour and tried to enhance the boring persona
I used to be determined to be.

Keep me at arm's length

I think the self-awareness was driving us partially insane,
The only time we were good for each other was when we weren't romantically together,
But then when we confided in one another in a platonic sort of way,
There was nothing I wanted more than to have you with me every day.

We still said things we shouldn't say,
I love you's were still part of our common way to depart from one another,
Even when we said those words with full utter desire,
Desire that remained,
After all these years we quit trying to be something that was no longer salvageable.

It drove me crazy to have you in my life,
Because I could never be with you without destroying who we are,
But if you ever fell in love again with someone who wasn't me,
Well, I'd curse myself each day
That I let you go even though I know you've already been freed.

Lie to me

We lie so much that we've forgotten how to tell the truth,
In a bed we stay at night,
Next to each other
But worlds apart.

We smile as if it's normal and we don't want to rip each other's faces off,
And we stay in a house and don't leave
Except for the few hours we aren't together.

Stay with me and lie for the rests of our lives
Because it keeps the peace,
Even when I know there are secrets you like to hide in the dark.

We've become detached lovers,
Separated from honesty,
With a low chance of compatibility,
But I count on your presence
And I know you would miss my body heat.

Unbreakable bonds

I was always told that certain bonds could never be broken,
You were drawn to them forever,
For it was a simple fact over matter.

The longer I tried to hold onto these bonds
Meant the more I felt torn between living,
There was no common decency
Or love I could feel on the other end,
It was knowing that in these relations
I'd only be giving without ever receiving.

I wanted no strings drawn to me,
And to break everyone free,
Bonds could be changeable,
So why are we pretending to be
With people that ignore us
And feel as if they are allowed to constantly critique?

My anatomy

If you broke me down into smaller parts,
All you ever used to see was atoms floating
With no particular reason for moving.

Now every part of me,
Tells a story of you,
Each molecule inside of my body
Was awoken with purpose.

It was all because every fibre of my being
Now knew exactly what to do,
Which was to undeniably love you.

Mess me up

You told me you would only ruin me,
I told you I didn't care
Because somehow I didn't think you were capable of it,
I only knew what I wanted
And that was you.

All I needed was to be lucky,
You choosing me made me feel that,
And even though you thought you were a disturbance,
Being with you was my greatest occurrence.

A home away from you

I built a better home
Far away from you,
A place where I didn't mask how I expressed,
Roofs built high with my designs,
A place where I could love myself,
Safe and sound from all of your external hatred
That you never tried to hide.

It had a fence to keep you out,
But I saw you there one day
Trying to invade,
The things I left you out from,
You banged and screamed but I held on tight,
I protected my new home with all my might.

You walked away and left my space alone,
I wondered if that made you hurt,
Seeing me take my final step,
One without you,
If it did it didn't show.

That day we said goodbye to everything we'd ever been,
Every stage we fought on and laughed till we died,
We grew till we could be no taller,
And that frightened you.

So you tried to cut me down
But I ran and didn't look back.

I turned solo and shut you out,
Then you shrunk and realised your mistake,
That we could've been bigger no matter our sizes.

Awkward silences

I ran out of words
And interesting things to say,
It was all an act and I became tired
Of every conversation that was made.

We talked too much without saying anything,
Never caught up in any meanings
Or what words we held back every day.

Our words were just fillers
That were spoken with no consideration
With an effortless careless annotation.

I missed our old exchanges,
Where we looked at each other with never ending curiosity
And said words that made our hearts thump and our eyes widen,
Interactions ended with goodbyes
And excitement for the next time that we associated.

Every good morning you said to me,
Was said with less care,
Because you hated repetition
But I never thought you would grow wary of me
Soon enough it became clear to see that even I
Just became another reason why you hated routines.

Your shadow

You could achieve anything,
I'd still watch,
Devoid of any substance
Because I felt everything through you.

You could do things that I never could,
I was always just frozen with fear,
But I'd act as your light,
To make everyone pay attention,
Because even though no one ever saw me
You were one of those people worth being seen.

I was never a natural at anything,
There were no obvious talents I possessed,
Everything was tried
Except nothing ever worked out.

It gave me some sort of peace to know that the difference between us,
Was not that I didn't try,
But because I wasn't you.

How can we be friends now?

We made an agreement to each other,
It started when you convinced me we were both in situations we didn't want to be in,
I couldn't believe my luck when you told me you had feelings for me too.
So much so that my feelings couldn't be contained
Because I had waited eternities for you to say that.

The only problem was that we were both tied to other people, but neither of our circumstances were remarkable to say the least.
So we made a deal to free ourselves for love and finally be who we always desired
To be.

On the day we had our plan set I followed it through,
I hurt someone for you to still want me,
My feet walked up to your welcome mat and with courage I stayed.
Everything felt uncertain for I didn't know how you treated someone you might kiss
And proclaim.

There was no music, only the sounds of my whole body beating.

When the door began to creak and open my destiny
every hope I had inside me cracked,
And I was stripped into my own internal disbelief.

A girl stood before me,
The same one that held your hand for some time now.
She smiled,
And I glimpsed at what she was wearing,
It was the shirt you wore yesterday when you saw me.

The king of you heart

For a day I wanted to be the king of your love,
To own your heart
And be in control of what you felt,
Or know how to be able to make you fall apart.

There was so many ways in our normal life
That you had full domination over the ways we interacted,
But for once I wished I could throw you in the deep end,
Just so that you would question if I felt anything for you,
Rather than me always being consumed with overthinking
And hope that you liked me.

Nothing was ever obvious with you,
You fought with everything in you to keep every emotion concealed,
But you knew that you made me crazy,
And the fact that you did nothing about it
Was getting harder to acknowledge the more that we remained
Under a nameless label.

Will I ever see you again?

When we gave each other space,
Did you miss me a little?
Or do I no longer fit anywhere in your places?

Did you realise the little things we implemented in our routines?
Or do you not notice that I squeezed them in
So that you would remember me?

I would never say any indecent words when describing you,
Because even though I fell into all sorts of out of it
The day that you left,
You were good to me
And I wanted to thank you for taking care of flimsy heart.

Play me

If I was a song,
How would you play me?
I wanted to feel what I would sound like as music
Through your perception.

Would you play me loud
Or like a quiet melody?
Am I long or are the notes annoyingly short?
Does it give people goose bumps?
Would it make someone cry at the meaning?

If I were a song,
I wouldn't ever want you to stop playing me.
I'd want to be the one melody your fingers never forget,
The tune you go to play when someone wants to hear
How talented you are,
Or in a moment when you just want to forget everything.

Temporary crush

It fascinates me how much romantic tension
I thought was between us
When I had just imagined it all.

Every small inconsequential comment you made,
My head took too seriously,
Convinced that you were yearning for me in the same way.

I ignored the way you looked at other people
And told myself that I was special to you,
That you didn't talk to other people
Like you did with me.

But after months my intense feelings
Changed and I stopped liking the storying line
Because I think my feelings were only temporary,
Or partially me trying to cope with how
You were the one person that didn't make me feel so abnormal.

You don't like me anymore

I'm sorry that you stayed,
I should have indefinitely let you go when I had the chance,
Now you hide in frames,
Your miserable smile
That you cover with a laugh.

Who does it benefit when you stay for the wrong reasons,
The muscles to the curve of your mouth have long
forgotten the feeling of twitching upwards,
Noticing that
Could have ended me right away,
Because I never wanted to be the one that forced you into
remaining
In my affections.

It hurt that we would never grow old together
Since as much as I'd happily oblige,
You've now forgotten what it's like to be happy with me.

Can I exist in your eyes?

I never felt like I was a good person,
But meeting you
Was the closest I'd ever come to having good things.

I'd take away my voice just for you to hear me
And to be the centre of one your thoughts.
It drove me part mad that I never got the ability to read minds,
Because I was in desperate need to see if you didn't think
I was who everyone made me out to be all the time.

All of my ambitions had gone out the window when I got to know you,
There was no one else I wanted to meet,
You were it for me,
And it split apart my whole entire body
When none of my questions ever got a reply.

After all of this,
Would I still be someone you considered memorable?
Do you look at me as the only thing you can take whole?

Any clarity would make me feel like less of a fool
Because
You make me feel complete serenity.
Even your name reminded me of every cheesy melody.

Strangers

When I first realised that we became strangers
Was when my
First extinct to seeing you
Was to pretend you didn't exist,
Rather than ask you how you've been.

Can't be hidden

It was scary to be known so well by a person,
I don't know when you completely figured me out
But it terrified me that you did,
Because it just meant that you knew every fear that I had admitted.

Sometimes I wish I could reintroduce myself to you,
And learn how to hide at least some parts of me
Just so that when you left
I could make peace with knowing
That you didn't know every single thing that moulded me together.

Now when you put space between us,
It hurts more than it ever could
Because there aren't any qualities in me that I could acknowledge
That you weren't aware of.

So now if you broke me,
I'd be left raw knowing that you saw every fraction
And it still wasn't enough
To make the one I love
Not run away.

Our time left

There were a million reasons I could name
That were fair enough excuses as to why we didn't fit,
They all sounded the same and were easily fired down
But I couldn't keep pretending that I would ever be worth
having you.

You were bright and electric,
And deserving of someone that made your face beam
I couldn't keep fantasising that I could be that.
Because it was only destroying me completely by the minute
Bracing myself for when I would eventually watch you meet
The one you would inevitably end with.

Then you would realise everything I tried to warn you about
And I'd get the heart filled apologies
That claimed they could have never seen this coming
When I could have saved myself the heartbreak
By letting you pass me by.

Keep you in my pocket

If I ever disappear for a while, I promise to take you into my dimensions,
You hated being out of the loop
But I never knew that you felt left behind.
You were always running ahead of me in my mind,
Which is why it shocked me when you noticed the parts of my brain
That constantly spaced out.

Now that I have the choice to do things with company,
I'm scared I'll have to go back,
But for now it's nice to know we'd follow each other anywhere,
Which makes me think no one's ever been as close to me
As you have managed to become.

Music to my ears

Your laughter was the only sound I wanted to hear,
The wide spread of your lips the only thing I wished to witness,
I wasn't a comedian by far,
But my punchlines always had you releasing my favourite noise,
Which felt like heaven had reached my ears.

One of my biggest fears was
To think that one day you might get sick of looking at me,
Because honestly you were my favourite reason to be breathing,
Who else would I try to impress
If you were to one day turn a blind eye?

We may not have this forever,
Which had me already reminiscing
In case whoever I was in the future,
Had forgotten what it felt like to be loved by you.

Outsider

Human behaviour
Was never something I could understand,
It left me out of the loop,
Always forced to play an act,
Pretending that I understood what people were saying
And that their jokes were funny.

I did anything to not be an outsider,
Or labelled as an odd one.

No forced expression I tried to master
Worked well enough,
And no matter how many times I tried to start afresh,
Learning how to control what sides of me I showed to others,
It always ended the same:
Me regretting every choice of words I had muttered.

When was it my turn to feel normal
Or to meet people that didn't make me play pretend?
How long would I have to suffer in spaces with people that I couldn't get along with?
Why was it always me trying so hard
And never the other way around?

Keep talking

No one really talks to me,
Which is why I latched on so hard when you decided I was worth your time,
I was too afraid to be left alone again
Because I had no other person to speak to if you were to go away.

It was depressing the way I depended on you for companionship,
But I just didn't want to go back to talking to myself
And spending special occasions isolated.

Secrets within us

We were just kids,
When we got hit with aggressions we couldn't deal with,
What are we supposed to do now when there is this bursting space between us
And we don't know how to say the words that need to be said?

You know every inch of me,
So why now do we stray whenever one of us is near,
Hiding in the depths of the dark
Rather than get over our fear
And remember what it felt like
When we could never be torn apart.

I miss you when you aren't here,
But now it seems we've forgotten the act of what we considered normal.
So we ache in sorrow that not one of us is breaking first
And we live with tension,
That reminds us what we are yet to have.

You're my story

Lyrics were never enough to portray you,
Poems had yet been crafted with the beauty of you,
Movies failed to express everything you meant to me.

You were simply a feeling that only I
Would ever have the privilege of fully knowing.

To be your air

Everything that was near you,
I was constantly jealous of.
You were never close to me
But you were striking,
Something I had never seen.
My eyes had a mind of their own and immediately tracked your movements,
And what they found
Was always you in a picture-perfect scene.

It seemed that you were permanently shaped in breathtaking beauty,
Your surroundings were always obedient to you
By accentuating your every move,
Making it harder to breathe whenever we had shared the same space
Because I could never compete with such loveliness that engulfed your entire being.

I accepted that I could only ever gaze at you from a distance,
As I was afraid that if you were ever to be touched by me
You would shatter from my filth.

Floating through life you went,
Built as an antique

Watched by thousands who couldn't compare.

I was a used product not capable of being renewed,
But I would view you from the shelf I was placed on
Because you were worth the attention.

A night you'll forget

It was one of those nights
Where we laughed so hard that we forgot why we cried.
Stolen alcohol bottles from our parents
Hanged loosely in our hands,
The music was pumping loudly,
Filled with songs we didn't like.

Boys we wanted to kiss were out in the lawn,
Midnight skies were above us,
While we were too scared to check the time.

Hours had flown by and no one's thinking about tomorrow,
We're all just acting on impulses
And downing things to make us unconscious.

There wasn't hate, only sloppy expressions,
Nothing mattered.
Every agony and curse was forgotten,
We experienced the moment as it was
And we were reverted back to simple beings.

Saviour complex

He loved the idea of saving people,
But failed to see that not everyone needed him
And that people could rescue themselves.

It was as if he thrived when there were others that were suffering,
Because he wanted to feel special and needed
In a way that was guaranteed to not give him lasting friendships.

The problem that was always faced
Was when some of them figured out how to recover on their own,
Since he then wanted no part in their lives,
Only because he felt useless.

His attachments felt insufferable as they solely worked when one of them was dying,
But he never knew how to how to stay when there was a bright light.
So
What the boy did was stand on a waiting dock
Looking out on a telescope
Until he could find a body that was in desperate need of his attention.

Old lovers at the tombstone

It's another one those cold melancholy days, your eyes are roaming where I've laid for three years from today. Tears have nestled into your face, where they have remained for all these periods that have passed. Your fingers ache to touch the engraving of my name on the grainy tombstone, I'm just a floating ghost stuck with my only mission being to watch over you. We sit here together except you can't see me; we are two souls one transparent the other solid. Bearing this day in my weightless hands I can tell you have things to say and I'm not prepared for what I think they may mean. A mouth opens and words tumble out, they're horrible words and I want you take them back, but they're out and you can't see me so all I can do is subside in this invisible agony. I should be happy for you because you've found somebody else, I'm the one that left you ripped and made you a heartless person. She's waiting at your house supposedly, she'll never come close to me apparently, but still you have moved on, now I'm nothing but a painful memory and you'll start visiting less while you are caught up in another girl. Stuck on the earth I will haunt away, remembering that my first love now has a second.

Where you might go

If I asked you to leave it all behind,
Be someone to me,
And leave every omen that held us down,
Would you
Because it was an easy choice?

We always pretended to run,
Our shadows following in the same direction,
But never do we do any of it in meaning.

What if we recreated every dream we ever spoke about?
Said truths that were too scary to deny?

You lie in the dark with me every night
And your body trembles with fear that we'll always be trapped in this town,
But I'd build a plane just to get you out,
I'd let you leave me behind,
Just to know you had escaped our traitorous past.

Resurrected

Coming in to this world again,
I walked through doors that were shaped differently,
Stumbled my way into clumsy encounters
And looked at you as if you were everything.

Each particle that I was made up of had been reborn
With one common factor –
They lingered with desperate passion,
Wondering if your hands would fit in mine
And clung onto the feeling that us together is something we don't have to hide.

If you allowed me to,
I'd do it all,
Any inch of you that you gave me
Would be a gift I couldn't possibly take for granted.

All you were
Was an imperfect soul,
You had your troubles,
As did I,
But we could be flawed together and live in this new world,
Sharing secrets and holding each other tight.